1 PIANO, 4 HANDS

PIANO DUET PLAY·ALONG
VOLUME 23

COLE PORTER

Cover photo courtesy of Cole Porter Trust

ISBN 978-1-4234-3995-0

HAL·LEONARD®
CORPORATION
7777 W. BLUEMOUND RD. P.O. BOX 13819 MILWAUKEE, WI 53213

Visit Hal Leonard Online at
www.halleonard.com

CONTENTS

Page	Title	CD Track Secondo	CD Track Primo
4	ANOTHER OP'NIN', ANOTHER SHOW from *Kiss Me, Kate*	1	2
14	EASY TO LOVE from *Born to Dance*	3	4
22	FROM THIS MOMENT ON from *Out of This World*	5	6
30	I LOVE PARIS from *Can-Can* and *High Society*	7	8
36	I LOVE YOU from *Mexican Hayride*	9	10
44	I'VE GOT YOU UNDER MY SKIN from *Born to Dance*	11	12
52	IN THE STILL OF THE NIGHT from *Rosalie* and *Night and Day*	13	14
60	IT'S DE-LOVELY from *Red, Hot and Blue!*	15	16
70	SO IN LOVE from *Kiss Me, Kate*	17	18
80	YOU'D BE SO NICE TO COME HOME TO from *Something to Shout About*	19	20

ANOTHER OP'NIN', ANOTHER SHOW

from KISS ME, KATE

SECONDO

Words and Music by
COLE PORTER

ANOTHER OP'NIN', ANOTHER SHOW

from KISS ME, KATE

PRIMO

Words and Music by
COLE PORTER

SECONDO

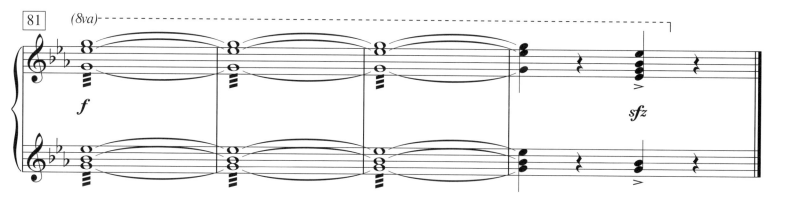

EASY TO LOVE
(You'd Be So Easy to Love)
from BORN TO DANCE

SECONDO

Words and Music by
COLE PORTER

EASY TO LOVE
(You'd Be So Easy to Love)
from BORN TO DANCE

PRIMO

Words and Music by
COLE PORTER

SECONDO

FROM THIS MOMENT ON

from OUT OF THIS WORLD

SECONDO

Words and Music by
COLE PORTER

FROM THIS MOMENT ON
from OUT OF THIS WORLD

PRIMO

Words and Music by
COLE PORTER

SECONDO

I LOVE PARIS

from CAN-CAN
from HIGH SOCIETY

SECONDO

Words and Music by
COLE PORTER

I LOVE PARIS

from CAN-CAN
from HIGH SOCIETY

PRIMO

Words and Music by
COLE PORTER

SECONDO

PRIMO

I LOVE YOU
from MEXICAN HAYRIDE

SECONDO

Words and Music by
COLE PORTER

Andante con moto

I LOVE YOU

from MEXICAN HAYRIDE

PRIMO

Words and Music by
COLE PORTER

I'VE GOT YOU UNDER MY SKIN

from BORN TO DANCE

SECONDO

Words and Music by
COLE PORTER

I'VE GOT YOU UNDER MY SKIN

from BORN TO DANCE

PRIMO

Words and Music by
COLE PORTER

SECONDO

PRIMO

SECONDO

PRIMO

IN THE STILL OF THE NIGHT

from ROSALIE
from NIGHT AND DAY

SECONDO

Words and Music by
COLE PORTER

IN THE STILL OF THE NIGHT

from ROSALIE
from NIGHT AND DAY

PRIMO

Words and Music by
COLE PORTER

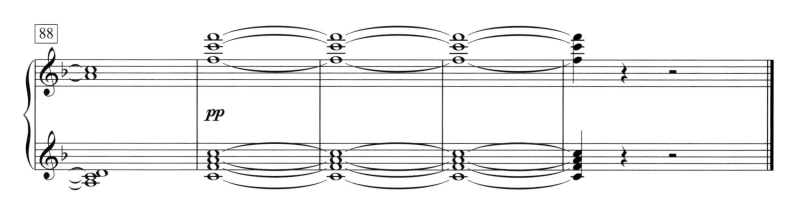

IT'S DE-LOVELY
from RED, HOT AND BLUE!

SECONDO

Words and Music by
COLE PORTER

IT'S DE-LOVELY
from RED, HOT AND BLUE!

PRIMO

Words and Music by
COLE PORTER

SECONDO

SO IN LOVE

from KISS ME, KATE

SECONDO

Words and Music by
COLE PORTER

SO IN LOVE
from KISS ME, KATE

PRIMO

Words and Music by
COLE PORTER

YOU'D BE SO NICE TO COME HOME TO
from SOMETHING TO SHOUT ABOUT

SECONDO

Words and Music by
COLE PORTER

YOU'D BE SO NICE TO COME HOME TO
from SOMETHING TO SHOUT ABOUT

PRIMO

Words and Music by
COLE PORTER

SECONDO

PRIMO

PIANO DUET PLAY·ALONG

The Piano Duet Play-Along series gives you the flexibility to rehearse or perform piano duets anytime, anywhere! Play these delightful tunes with a partner, or use the accompanying CDs to play along with either the Secondo or Primo part on your own. The audio CD is playable on any CD player, and also enhanced so PC and Mac users can adjust the recording to any tempo without changing pitch.

For More Information, See Your Local Music Dealer, or Write To:

HAL•LEONARD®
CORPORATION

7777 W. Bluemound Rd. P.O. Box 13819 Milwaukee, WI 53213

Disney characters and artwork are © Disney Enterprises, Inc.

1. Piano Favorites
9 great duets: Candle in the Wind • Chopsticks • Don't Know Why • Edelweiss • Goodbye Yellow Brick Road • Heart and Soul • Let It Be • Linus and Lucy • Your Song.

00290546 Book/CD Pack $14.95

2. Movie Favorites
8 classics: Chariots of Fire • The Entertainer • Theme from Jurassic Park • My Father's Favorite • My Heart Will Go On (Love Theme from Titanic) • Somewhere in Time • Somewhere, My Love • Star Trek® the Motion Picture.

00290547 Book/CD Pack $14.95

3. Broadway for Two
10 songs from the stage: Any Dream Will Do • Blue Skies • Cabaret • Climb Ev'ry Mountain • If I Loved You • Oklahoma • Ol' Man River • On My Own • There's No Business Like Show Business • What'll I Do?

00290548 Book/CD Pack $14.95

4. The Music of Andrew Lloyd Webber™
10 great duets: Close Every Door • Everything's Alright • I Don't Know How to Love Him • Love Changes Everything • Memory • The Music of the Night • Pie Jesu • Superstar • Unexpected Song • With One Look.

00290549 Book/CD Pack $14.95

5. Disney Favorites
8 songs: Bibbidi-Bobbidi-Boo (The Magic Song) • Can You Feel the Love Tonight • A Dream Is a Wish Your Heart Makes • Hakuna Matata • Reflection • Someday • A Spoonful of Sugar • You've Got a Friend in Me.

00290550 Book/CD Pack $14.95

6. Disney Songs
7 duets: Candle on the Water • Colors of the Wind • Feed the Birds • Go the Distance • Kiss the Girl • You'll Be in My Heart (Pop Version) • Zip-A-Dee-Doo-Dah.

00290551 Book/CD Pack $14.95

7. Classical Music
9 classical favorites: Ave Maria (Schubert) • Canon in D (Pachelbel) • Dance of the Sugar Plum Fairy (Tchaikovsky) • Fingal's Cave Overture (Mendelssohn) • Funeral March of a Marionette (Gounod) • Humoresque (Dvořák) • Jesu, Joy of Man's Desiring (Bach) • Piano Concerto No. 21 in C Major (Mozart) • Sleeping Beauty Waltz (Tchaikovsky).

00290552 Book/CD Pack $14.95

8. Christmas Classics
10 holiday songs: Blue Christmas • The Chipmunk Song • The Christmas Song (Chestnuts Roasting on an Open Fire) • Christmas Time Is Here • I'll Be Home for Christmas • It's Beginning to Look Like Christmas • Mistletoe and Holly • Rockin' Around the Christmas Tree • Rudolph the Red-Nosed Reindeer • Silver Bells • and more.

00290554 Book/CD Pack $14.95

9. Hymns
10 sacred favorites: Abide with Me • Amazing Grace • Beautiful Savior • Crown Him with Many Crowns • Fairest Lord Jesus • Holy, Holy, Holy! Lord God Almighty • The Old Rugged Cross • Onward, Christian Soldiers • Rock of Ages • What a Friend We Have in Jesus.

00290556 Book/CD Pack $14.95

10. The Sound of Music
10 beloved songs from the musical: Climb Ev'ry Mountain • Do-Re-Mi • Edelweiss • The Lonely Goatherd • Maria • My Favorite Things • Sixteen Going on Seventeen • So Long, Farewell • Something Good • The Sound of Music.

00290557 Book/CD Pack $16.95

11. Disney Early Favorites
10 great Disney duets: Give a Little Whistle • Heigh-Ho • Hi-Diddle-Dee-Dee (An Actor's Life for Me) • I'm Wishing • I've Got No Strings • Some Day My Prince Will Come • When I See an Elephant Fly • When You Wish upon a Star • Whistle While You Work • Who's Afraid of the Big Bad Wolf?

00290558 Book/CD Pack $16.95

12. Disney Movie Songs
9 well-known songs: The Bare Necessities • Be Our Guest • Chim Chim Cher-ee • Circle of Life • Cruella De Vil • God Help the Outcasts • If I Never Knew You (Love Theme from Pocahontas) • Part of Your World • A Whole New World.

00290559 Book/CD Pack $16.95

13. Movie Hits
8 film favorites: Theme from E.T. (The Extra-Terrestrial) • Forrest Gump – Main Title (Feather Theme) • The Godfather (Love Theme) • The John Dunbar Theme • Moon River • Romeo and Juliet (Love Theme) • Theme from Schindler's List • Somewhere, My Love.

00290560 Book/CD Pack $14.95

14. Les Misérables
8 great songs from the musical: Bring Him Home • Castle on a Cloud • Do You Hear the People Sing? • A Heart Full of Love • I Dreamed a Dream • In My Life • On My Own • Stars.

00290561 Book/CD Pack $16.95

15. God Bless America® & Other Songs for a Better Nation
8 patriotic duets: America, the Beautiful • Anchors Aweigh • Battle Hymn of the Republic • Climb Ev'ry Mountain • God Bless America • God Bless the U.S.A. • This Is My Country • What a Wonderful World.

00290562 Book/CD Pack $14.95

16. Disney Classics
10 favorites: Alice in Wonderland • The Ballad of Davy Crockett • Beauty and the Beast • It's a Small World • Lavender Blue (Dilly Dilly) • Little April Shower • Mickey Mouse March • Once upon a Dream • Supercalifragilisticexpialidocious • Under the Sea.

00290563 Book/CD Pack $16.95

17. High School Musical
9 songs from the TV hit production: Bop to the Top • Breaking Free • Get'cha Head in the Game • I Can't Take My Eyes Off of You • Start of Something New • Stick to the Status Quo • We're All in This Together • What I've Been Looking For • When There Was Me and You.

00290564 Book/CD Pack $16.95

18. High School Musical 2
8 songs from the sequel: All for One • Everyday • Fabulous • Gotta Go My Own Way • I Don't Dance • What Time Is It • Work This Out • You Are the Music in Me.

00290565 Book/CD Pack $16.95

19. Pirates of the Caribbean
9 pieces: The Black Pearl • Brethren Court • He's a Pirate • Jack Sparrow • The Kraken • The Medallion Calls • One Day • Up Is Down • Wheel of Fortune.

00290566 Book/CD Pack $16.95

20. Wicked
8 selections from this Broadway hit: Dancing Through Life • Defying Gravity • For Good • I Couldn't Be Happier • I'm Not That Girl • Popular • What Is This Feeling? • The Wizard and I.

00290567 Book/CD Pack $16.95

21. Peanuts®
8 tunes from this animated classic: Blue Charlie Brown • Charlie Brown Theme • The Great Pumpkin Waltz • Joe Cool • Linus and Lucy • Oh, Good Grief • Red Baron • You're in Love, Charlie Brown.

00290568 Book/CD Pack $16.95

22. Rodgers & Hammerstein
10 songs from this dynamic duo: Do I Love You Because You're Beautiful? • Happy Talk • Hello, Young Lovers • I Whistle a Happy Tune • If I Loved You • My Favorite Things • People Will Say We're in Love • Some Enchanted Evening • The Surrey with the Fringe on Top • You'll Never Walk Alone.

00290569 Book/CD Pack $14.95

23. Cole Porter
10 tunes from the legendary composer: Another Op'nin', Another Show • Easy to Love (You'd Be So Easy to Love) • From This Moment On • I Love Paris • I Love You • I've Got You Under My Skin • In the Still of the Night • It's De-Lovely • So in Love • You'd Be So Nice to Come Home To.

00290570 Book/CD Pack $14.95

24. Christmas Carols
9 holiday favorites: Angels We Have Heard on High • Ding Dong! Merrily on High! • The First Noel • God Rest Ye Merry, Gentlemen • Hark! the Herald Angels Sing • It Came upon the Midnight Clear • O Come, All Ye Faithful (Adeste Fideles) • O Little Town of Bethlehem • What Child Is This?

00290571 Book/CD Pack $14.95